Start TO Finish
Second Series

FROM Garbage TO Compost

LISA OWINGS

LERNER PUBLICATIONS Minneapolis

Copyright © 2017 by Lerner Publishing Group, Inc.

Lerner Publications Company
A division of Lerner Publishing Group, Inc.
241 First Avenue North
Minneapolis, MN 55401 USA

For reading levels and more information, look up this title at www.lernerbooks.com.

Library of Congress Cataloging-in-Publication Data

Names: Owings, Lisa, author.
Title: From garbage to compost / Lisa Owings.
Other titles: Start to finish (Minneapolis, Minn.). Second series.
Description: Minneapolis : Lerner Publications, [2016] | Series: Start to finish. second series | Audience: Ages 5–9. | Audience: K to grade 3. | Includes bibliographical references and index.
Identifiers: LCCN 2015036496| ISBN 9781512409116 (lb : alk. paper) | ISBN 9781512412994 (pb : alk. paper) | ISBN 9781512410839 (eb pdf)
Subjects: LCSH: Compost—Juvenile literature. | Organic wastes—Recycling—Juvenile literature.
Classification: LCC S661 .O95 2016 | DDC 631.8/75—dc23

LC record available at http://lccn.loc.gov/2015036496

Manufactured in the United States of America
1 – CG – 7/15/16

TABLE OF Contents

Compost helps my garden! How is it made?

First, gardeners find a place for compost.

A good place for a compost bin is on bare soil where it will get partial sun. It should be somewhere **convenient** to add to and care for. Gardeners can make or buy compost bins.

Next, they sort their garbage.

Not all garbage can be composted. Gardeners save most kitchen scraps and some paper products for composting. But items like leftover meat and dairy or plastics and chemicals can't be composted.

Then they add garden waste.

Gardeners collect their grass clippings, plant trimmings, and fallen leaves. They try not to include weed seeds or plants with **diseases**. Both of these can spread to the garden when the compost is used.

Gardeners use layers of waste and soil.

Layers of kitchen and garden waste are added until the compost bin is full. It is important to add soil too. The **microorganisms** in the soil help break down the compost.

Next, the pile is watered.

The compost pile needs to be kept moist but not sopping wet. The microorganisms need just enough water to survive.

The sun heats the compost.

The sun speeds up the composting process. Many of the microorganisms that break down compost need high temperatures to perform their best. Heat also helps kill any harmful pests, diseases, and **bacteria**.

Gardeners stir their compost.

Gardeners turn their compost regularly. This helps move oxygen through the pile. Most **decomposers** need oxygen to breathe and do their work, just as we do.

They wait for the compost to decompose.

Once it has all the basic ingredients, compost needs time to decompose. Gardeners can help it along by stirring it often and making sure it has the right amounts of water and heat.

Finally, the compost is ready to use!

After several months, the compost doesn't look like garbage at all. It looks like rich, dark soil. The finished compost is full of **nutrients**. Composting is an easy way to keep our planet green and clean!

Glossary

bacteria: tiny living things that are everywhere and can be harmful or helpful

compost: a decomposed mixture of garbage and garden waste that is used to help gardens grow

convenient: nearby and easy to get to

decompose: to decay or to be slowly broken down by natural processes

decomposers: insects, fungi, bacteria, or other organisms that break down organic material by feeding on it

diseases: illnesses. Diseases in compost can spread to the rest of the garden when compost is used.

microorganisms: living things that are so tiny they can be seen only through a microscope

nutrients: substances that plants, animals, and people need to live and be healthy

Further Information

Composting for Kids!
http://aggie-horticulture.tamu.edu/kindergarden/kidscompost
/CompostingForKids.pdf
This site has lots of details about how to make your own compost.

Cornell, Kari. *The Nitty-Gritty Gardening Book: Fun Projects for All Seasons.*
Minneapolis: Millbrook Press, 2015. Don't have a garden to use your compost?
This book has plenty of projects to help you develop your green thumb.

Lay, Richard. *A Green Kid's Guide to Composting.* Minneapolis: Magic
Wagon, 2013. Read this book for more tips about composting and chemical-
free gardening.

PBS Kids: Worm Farm
http://pbskids.org/dragonflytv/show/wormfarm.html
Ever heard of composting worms? Watch this video to learn about this wiggly
way of composting.

Index

Photo Acknowledgments
The images in this book are used with the permission of:
© Mona Makela/Shutterstock.com, p. 1; © Villiers Steyn/
Shutterstock.com, p. 3; © audaxl/Shutterstock.com, p. 5;
© JGI/Jamie Grill/Getty Images, p. 7; © Lakov Filimonov/
Shutterstock.com, p. 9; © Paul Mansfield/Getty Images,
p. 11; © Biosphoto/SuperStock, p. 13; © Evan Lorne/
Shutterstock.com, p. 15; © iStockphoto.com/cjp, p. 17;
© Rachel Husband/Alamy, p. 19; © Alison Hancock/
Shutterstock.com, p. 21.

Front cover: © Evan Lorne/Shutterstock.com.

Main body text set in Arta Std Book 20/26.
Typeface provided by International Typeface Corp.

LERNER e SOURCE™ Expand learning beyond the printed book. Download free, complementary educational resources for this book from our website, www.lerneresource.com.